Tabitha

Tabitha

The Story of a Much-Travelled Cat

Helen Harris

Photography by Jane Tirard

Book Guild Publishing
Sussex, England

Pr   d

A ̶   n

This is the story of a very beautiful tabby cat called Tabitha. Her fur is short and thick, basically sandy-coloured but with well-defined dark markings, some white around her mouth and in a small patch on her chest.

Tabitha's life started in England, in Kent where she and another kitten, a black one named Bramble, were acquired

by Mistress Jane to live in a house with a big garden in the country, amid apple and pear orchards. The two kittens were the same age, but from different litters, and they soon became firm friends. They would go out together and explore the nearby field, come back together, eat together, and sleep together . Sometimes they brought in little presents for their mistress, in the form of mice and voles – gifts that were not altogether joyfully received.

So tired

A cat flap was fitted in the kitchen window of the house so that Tabitha and Bramble could come and go as they wished. Each kitten was fitted with a collar containing an electronic device that activated the flap when either of them approached, but which prevented unwanted cats from entering.

Very sadly, after about a year Bramble met with a fatal accident – a collision with a car on the nearby road. Now the one-and-only cat, Tabitha became very affectionate to Mistress Jane, spending much more time sitting on her lap. She also developed her own independent lifestyle.

Tabitha – going to write her life story?

Like all cats, Tabitha loved to lie in the sun. She would stretch out on the patio or in the sun-room, and roll over onto her back, displaying the soft, light-brown, dark-spotted fur along her tummy. When she could, she made her way upstairs and settled on her mistress's bed. Mistress Jane was very fond of her, although she showed her displeasure when Tabitha tried to catch birds in the garden. Tabitha would wait for her mistress to come home from work, and would soon be curled up on her lap, purring, while Jane enjoyed a cup of tea.

Tabitha liked to go and spend time hunting in the neighbouring field, where some horses grazed. But one day she came home with blood on her face. She sat at the open back door feeling sorry for herself, and her face slowly became very swollen. Mistress Jane was very concerned so she took Tabitha to the vet. He examined her carefully but could find no broken bones, and thought that poor Tabitha might have been kicked by one of the horses. The vet advised that she should spend the next few days very quietly, and fortunately she soon recovered. But she was always wary of horses after that.

Tabitha had to be taken to the vet at other times, for various purposes such as injections, and she didn't like it, although everyone was very kind. What really annoyed her was being bundled into the carrying-box, and she always protested at such an affront to her dignity.

Sometimes Mistress Jane would have to be away for a few days, and then kind friends would come in to feed Tabitha, stroke her and have a talk. Tabitha had her toys to play with – plastic ping-pong balls, and a pretend mouse which she could toss around and pounce on. She also had a scratching post, which she liked to sharpen her front claws on. This meant that she did not attack the carpets and furniture.

When Tabitha was about five years old a ginger tom cat came around from next door, when a new dog was introduced there that he did not like. Because he seemed to have abandoned his former home, he was having to hunt for his food and had become thin. Mistress Jane took pity on him and started feeding him outside the house. Tabitha did not like him at all – she would spit and chase him away. As this upset Tabitha, Jane advertised for a new owner, and a kind lady came and took him on, and gave him a good home.

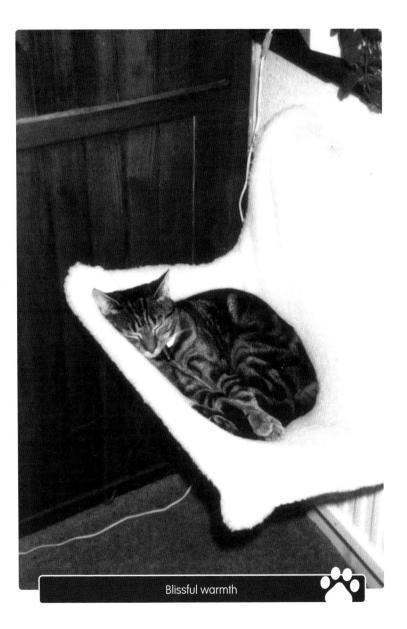

Blissful warmth

When Tabitha was nine years old and had grown into a nice plump pussycat, Mistress Jane had to move, to work in America. She really didn't want to be parted from Tabitha and, after asking advice from the vet, decided she should go with her. She then investigated all the requirements for the journey. Tabitha had to stay in a cattery near Heathrow airport for three to four days while Mistress Jane flew to the United States. There she prepared a place in the new house so that Tabitha could settle easily.

All preparations were made, and Miss Tabitha again had to submit to the indignity of a travel box – this time a large purpose-built crate – for the drive to the cattery. The day dawned for the flight across the Atlantic. Tabitha was put back in the crate and taken to the airport animal centre where she was comfortably accommodated with her own enclosed area, complete with all she needed. She was well cared for by the staff until it was time to board for the seven-hour journey. Cats are not normally sedated

A frequent pastime

Waiting for lunch?

for long flights, but are kept under the care of the flight crew in a separate hold for animals. Tabitha found that she was sharing the hold with several rabbits – fortunately securely segregated. On arrival at Detroit she hardly knew she was in a different country, especially when she saw Mistress Jane again and was driven from the airport to their new house.

Her new home was in the state of Michigan. The house had big windows and there was a good-sized garden, backing on to a golf course. Tabitha quickly found her way around, investigating every corner and cranny. She soon discovered how enjoyable it was to roll over on the smooth wood floor

Cooling in the bushes

indoors as the sun streamed in, or outside on the warm, brick-paved patio. When the sun became too hot she would go underneath the bushes for shade, but sometimes, when the heat was excessive, Mistress Jane would bring her indoors to benefit from the air conditioning.

Sometimes Tabitha tracked down a chipmunk, a kind of tiny, stripey squirrel found in that area, and Mistress Jane was not at all pleased when she brought one of them into the house. In fact, on one occasion, a chipmunk stayed the night. Tabitha chased it around the house, slipping and sliding on the wood floors until it hid away. The next morning it appeared again, and eventually ran out through

the back door which Mistress Jane had left open.

Tabitha has always purred a lot, and she is a talkative cat. She readily gives a loud 'miaow' in greeting. She often spoke to Mistress Jane's mother on the telephone, her voice being carried across the Atlantic back to England.

In winter much snow falls in Michigan. Then Tabitha would spend most of her time indoors. She had her own place for sleeping and eating, but in the daytime she knew all the cosiest spots near the heating ducts where she could curl up. Any large paper bag or cardboard box that might be lying around prompted Tabitha's close investigation – she

would creep in, and sometimes settle for a little doze.

Tabitha has always had a taste for good food. Sometimes she put on extra weight around her tummy as she got older, and then her mistress had to be firm and restrict her diet

to prevent her becoming obese and unfit. After a few weeks these measures were usually effective and Tabitha regained her slim figure.

After some years, by which time Tabitha was fourteen

years old, Mistress Jane had to move to another part of America, to the state of Connecticut. Miss Tabitha sensed that something was afoot, as there was much coming and going and packing of things into boxes and cases. Then, her mistress told her, they had to make a journey together. Jane was to drive them in her car over 700 miles, in one stretch, to their new home. Tabitha watched as all kinds of luggage were packed into the car early in the morning, and as her carrying-box – a special one this time – was made snug for her. She wanted to cooperate as well as she could, and Mistress Jane was very pleased with her (and relieved) when Tabitha sensibly used her litter-tray just ten minutes before departure time. That ensured that she was comfortable for the long journey and could enjoy the music that played on the car stereo.

Before Mistress Jane found a more permanent home, she and Tabitha spent six months in temporary accommodation. This had an open-plan garden so Tabitha's outings to it had to be restricted to when Mistress Jane was at home. It was a very small place with no inside doors, so Tabitha had the run of the house. She liked to go upstairs to her mistress's bedroom, and in the night would miaow, purr and wake her up, which was not always appreciated.

Jane then bought a house about 30 miles away on the edge of a small town. Tabitha quickly became used to it – she has always been very adaptable. The house had no cat flap but Mistress Jane would let Tabitha out under her supervision for spells in the nice garden. The garden was surrounded by woods where there were wild deer. Tabitha was fascinated. She watched them intently, but kept her distance. She didn't see any other cats around as they tend to live indoors in America.

After about a year, although happy there, Mistress Jane decided to return to the United Kingdom. She sold the house, and again mistress and cat moved, this time to stay with friends for a few months. Here there were other animals to become acquainted with. One was a big black cat called Mr Spike, who had also originally come from England. To begin with, he and Tabitha did not like each

Kiwa

Bandit

Mr Spike

Tabitha's friends

Kiwa & Bandit

Tabitha and Mr Spike confront each other

other. Mr Spike seemed to resent this new cat on his territory, and they would yowl in disapproval. Eventually they settled into a state of mutual respect.

There were also some friendly dogs – two Jack Russells, a female called Bandit and a male called Kiwa. Tabitha got on particularly well with them, and they would sit together. When they were resting, Kiwa had a way of sitting with his front paws crossed, a habit that Tabitha appeared to pick up from him and which has stayed with her ever since.

As the time for Jane's return to England drew nearer, there were questions to consider. Would Tabitha, now aged fifteen, be able to withstand another big move, involving a further transatlantic flight? Jane hated the thought of leaving her dear furry companion, and after all Tabitha was very fit. Veterinary advice was sought, and Jane was told that there was no reason why Tabitha should not

Tabitha

accompany her. There was now an alternative to quarantine, involving a microchip and blood tests, so a programme, which took six months, was put in hand. This of course meant more of those vet visits, in which Tabitha was poked, prodded and pricked. It was not altogether pleasant but she behaved impeccably, and the vet proclaimed that all was well. She was healthy, and fit to travel.

The flight was booked. Miss Tabitha was able to travel on the same night flight as her mistress, but separately, and she had to be at the airport five hours before departure time. On the day, Jane's good friend Sue drove them the two-hour journey to Boston. The large 4 x 4 American vehicle was filled with luggage. Tabitha said goodbye to Mr Spike, Bandit and Kiwa, and was placed in the middle of it, in a new box. Penny, the good friend with whom they had stayed, waved farewell as, after seven happy years in the United States of America, Jane and Tabitha were driven away.

The time following their arrival at the airport was very stressful for Jane. Strict guidance is given regarding the measurements of an animal's travel-box, which Jane had observed. However, because Tabitha was so inquisitive and chose to sit up straight in the box to look around, the tips of her ears just touched its lid. This caused a problem with the officials which threatened to delay boarding until it was solved by Tabitha having to lose some of her cushions to give clearance. After leaving Tabitha at the special place designated for cargo, Jane had to wait until the flight was called. Then she looked out across the tarmac to the huge waiting aircraft in which Tabitha was already aboard, and she couldn't help feeling some concern.

Fortunately it was a fairly smooth flight, much to the relief of both Tabitha and Mistress Jane. On arrival at Heathrow Tabitha, in her box, was to leave the aircraft before other passengers and was due to remain at the airport for a

Catching up on sleep after the flight

Still climbing at age 16

possible three hours. After collecting her baggage, Jane made her way to the animal reception centre and was glad to hear that her cat was fine. She had travelled well on her own in the hold, and hadn't slept much, but with no problems and was ready to leave.

For her first year back in England Jane was to live in

another temporary house, in Surrey, and as soon as she had collected Tabitha this is where they went. Again Mistress Jane showed her the location of her litter tray, and her bed and food dishes. Tabitha inspected everything and gave her apparent approval. She was interested to note that the house's back door had a cat flap – like the one she had learned to use back in those days in Kent – so she was able to access the small garden at the rear whenever she wanted.

The garden was very pleasant, safely enclosed by walls and
fences, and with plenty of spots where she could enjoy
the sun.

At the end of the year Mistress Jane was appointed to a new
job, which meant a move to Berkshire and another road
journey – but not nearly as long as the one from Michigan

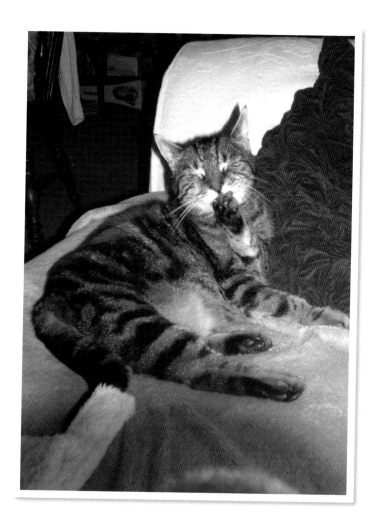

to Connecticut. By this time Tabitha had learned to take such moves in her stride.

Now an elderly lady, Tabitha has settled well again and still faces life with a relaxed dignity. Like many old ladies she snoozes quite a lot. She still purrs and speaks on the telephone, and enjoys the food Mistress Jane prepares for her. This includes, as daily treats, tasty pellets brought from America, and sometimes crumbs of fruit cake. Now and again she still has to endure a visit to the vet for a check-up. On returning home, Mistress Jane rewards her with her favourite delicacy – a king prawn. What more could a happy cat wish for?